EDGE
BOOKS

X-SPORTS

PAINTBALL

BY TERRI SIEVERT

CONSULTANT:
CHRIS RAEHL, PRESIDENT
NATIONAL COLLEGIATE PAINTBALL ASSOCIATION

Capstone press

Mankato, Minnesota

Edge Books are published by Capstone Press
151 Good Counsel Drive, P.O. Box 669, Mankato, Minnesota 56002
www.capstonepress.com

Library of Congress Cataloging-in-Publication Data
Sievert, Terri.
   Paintball / by Terri Sievert.
   p. cm.—(Edge books. X-sports)
   Includes bibliographical references and index.
   ISBN 0-7368-2711-0 (hardcover)
   1. Paintball (Game)—Juvenile literature. I. Title. II. Series.
GV1202.S87S54 2005
796.2—dc22   2004000505

Summary: Discusses the sport of paintball, including gear, strategies, and
   paintball tournaments.

Editorial Credits
Tom Adamson, editor; Jason Knudson, designer; Jo Miller, photo researcher;
   Eric Kudalis, product planning editor

Photo Credits
Capstone Press/Gary Sundermeyer, cover, 5, 6, 7, 9, 10, 11, 13 (both), 14, 15,
   23, 25 (both)
Darrin Johnson, 27, 29
Steven J. Meunier, 19, 20, 22

1 2 3 4 5 6 09 08 07 06 05 04

TABLE OF CONTENTS

_1/07_
Book Farm

CHAPTER 1

PAINTBALL

A player slowly looks around a barrier. His heart races. He sees the barrel of a paintball gun pointing at him. This is not what he wants to see. Splat! The player is hit with a paintball. A bright mark appears on his clothing. He is out of the game.

Paintball players try to mark other players with a paintball. They lurk behind barriers to keep themselves from being hit. Players hit by paintballs must leave the game.

Players describe paintball as safe danger. They are shot but not seriously hurt. Excitement builds as they try to survive the game without being hit.

LEARN ABOUT:

- Safe danger
- Capture the flag
- Speedball

Paintball players try to mark opponents with paintballs.

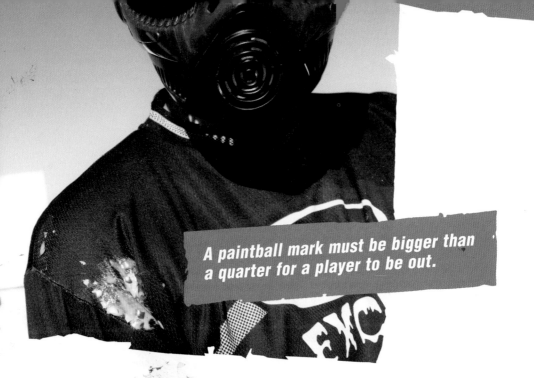

A paintball mark must be bigger than a quarter for a player to be out.

RECREATIONAL PAINTBALL

Recreational paintball is commonly played in a wooded area. Two teams usually play a game called capture the flag. Each team tries to take the other team's flag. A game often lasts 15 minutes or longer.

The size of a paintball team depends on the size of the playing field. A small field may have teams with four or five players. A large field can hold teams with hundreds of players.

EDGE FACT

Many paintball field owners only allow kids over age 10 to play.

COMPETITIVE PAINTBALL

Competitive paintball is usually called speedball. Speedball is played in a smaller area than paintball games in the woods. Players hide behind wood or inflated barriers. Three to seven players usually make up a team. Games can last three to 10 minutes.

Most speedball games are a form of capture the flag. Two teams try to get to a flag in the middle of the field. They have to bring the flag to the other team's flag station.

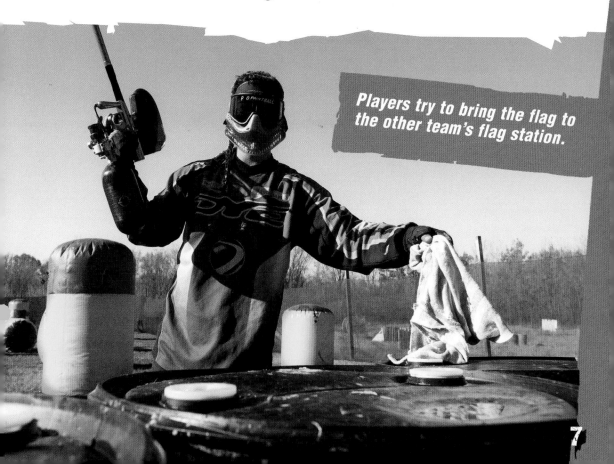

Players try to bring the flag to the other team's flag station.

CHAPTER 2

PAINTBALL GEAR

Paintball players need paintball guns and paintballs. They wear safety gear. Players can rent gear at paintball fields. Some players spend hundreds or thousands of dollars buying gear.

PAINTBALL GUNS

A paintball gun is called a marker. It fires paintballs. The paintballs usually break when they hit something.

Parts of a marker include the grip, hopper, trigger, and barrel. The player holds the marker with the grip. Paintballs go into the hopper. The player squeezes the trigger to send a paintball through the barrel and out of the gun.

LEARN ABOUT:

- Markers and paintballs
- Camouflage
- Safety gear

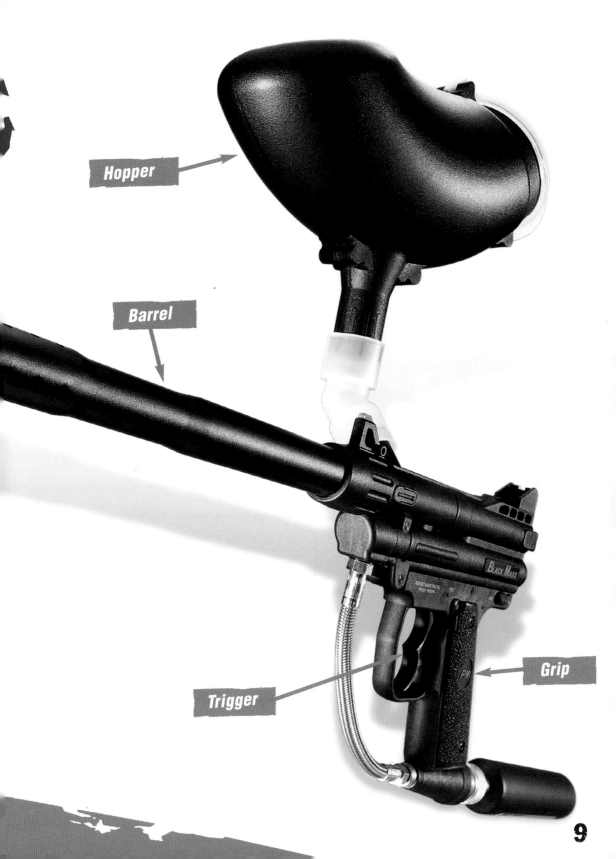

Hopper

Barrel

Trigger

Grip

9

Players must use a barrel sock when not playing.

Players put a barrel sock over the end of the barrel when they are not playing. A string holds the barrel sock in place. The sock prevents players from accidentally shooting a paintball. Players also put a sock over the barrel when they are out of the game.

EDGE FACT

The first paintguns were used in forestry to mark trees and by farmers to mark cows.

PAINTBALLS

Paintballs are round pellets. They are .68 inch (1.7 centimeters) across. The outside of the capsule is usually made of gelatin. The liquid inside isn't really paint. A colored liquid is used instead of paint. It can be washed off with soap and water. People still call them paintballs because the first markers did use real paint.

A paintball may break inside a player's gun. The player cleans the gun with a squeegee. A squeegee has a swab on a stick or cable.

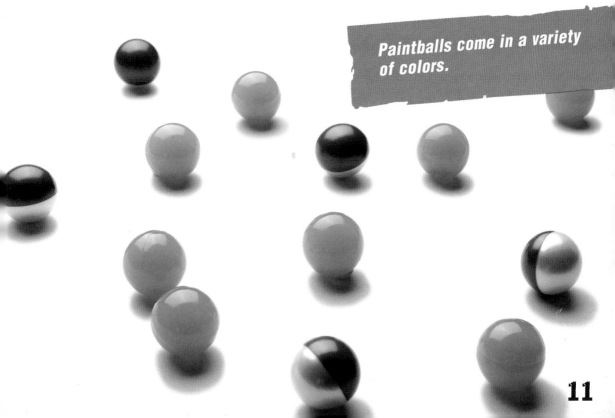

Paintballs come in a variety of colors.

HOPPERS

Paintballs are placed in a hopper on top of the gun. A hopper can usually hold about 200 paintballs.

A player squeezes the trigger to release a blast of compressed gas. The blast of gas pushes a paintball out of the gun. The gas is stored in an air tank on the back of the gun. The gas can be carbon dioxide, commonly called CO_2. Some markers have nitrogen or high-pressure air. High-pressure air is usually called HPA.

The paintball can travel up to 300 feet (91 meters) per second. This speed is the fastest the rules allow.

CLOTHING

In the woods, most players wear dark clothing. Camouflage clothing also helps a player hide in the woods. Bright colors are often worn for speedball games.

Players wear equipment for protection. Gloves protect the hands. It's painful when paintballs hit bare knuckles. Players may also wear knee pads and shin guards.

Paintballs are loaded into the gun's hopper.

Markers must be set so the paintballs travel less than 300 feet (91 meters) per second.

FPS / BPS

295

F = LOW BATTERY

PAINTBALL RADAR

Each team wears a different colored armband. Clothes cannot cover the armband. The color of the armband may match the color of the team's flag.

Many players wear a pack to carry extra paintballs. A pack is a belt with pouches. Players carry extra paintballs in the pouches.

Proper safety gear helps prevent injuries.

Goggles and a face mask protect a player's eyes and face.

GOGGLES

Players wear goggles to protect their eyes. Goggles are part of a face mask. The hard mask protects the sides of the head. The neck and front of the face are also protected.

Goggles with thermal lenses use two panes of strong clear plastic. The air between the panes prevents fogging. A coating also helps keep the lenses from getting foggy.

15

GEAR DIAGRAM

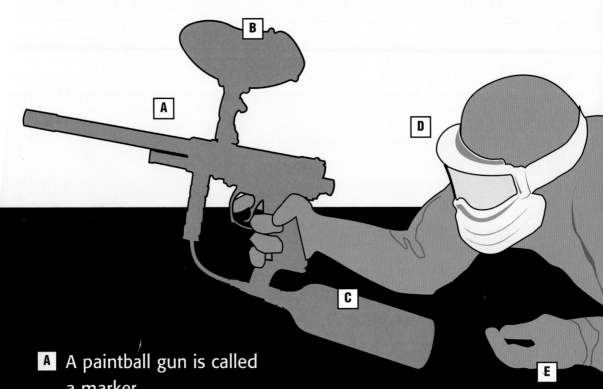

A A paintball gun is called a marker.

B The hopper holds the paintballs.

C The air tank holds the air that pushes the paintball out through the barrel.

D Players must wear goggles and a face mask.

E Players wear gloves to protect their hands.

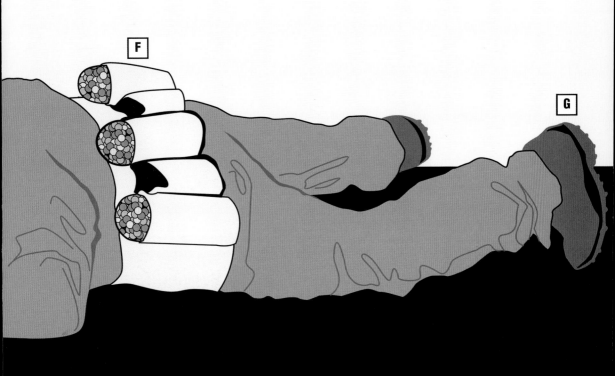

F Players carry extra
paintballs in a pack.

G Some players have
cleats on the bottom
of their shoes.

CHAPTER 3

PAINTBALL STRATEGY

Referees make sure people play by the rules. Referees wear striped or bright colored shirts. They tell a player if a paintball has made a mark.

Players who are hit yell, "I'm hit," or "I'm out." They must raise a hand or the paintgun over their head. Marked players can no longer talk to teammates.

GETTING STARTED

Teams can start the game in different ways. Players may move out quickly at the beginning of the game. They look for a spot from which to fire. Players should spread out when the game starts. Players bunched together are easy targets.

LEARN ABOUT:

- **Team strategy**
- **Player strategy**
- **Playing smart**

A marked player must raise a hand or the paintgun and say, "I'm out."

A team can take cover and wait for the other team to make its move.

Teams use different strategies. A team may send one player to rush the other team's side of the field. A team may send many players forward to surprise the other team. A team can also take cover on its side of the field. Team members then ambush the other team when opposing players try to take the flag.

A team may move down the field in a skirmish line. Players keep 10 to 12 feet (3 to 4 meters) between each player. A skirmish line makes it hard for the other team to get to the other side of the field.

PAINTBALL SLANG:

Newbie: a new player

Paint check: when a referee checks a player for a paint mark

Take it to the wire: go to the right or left side of the field

Walk-on: a player who does not have a reservation but is ready to play with others at the field

SCOUTS AND SNIPERS

A scout may go to the other team's side of the field alone. The scout tries to find out where the players on the other team are hiding.

A scout has to watch out for snipers. A player from the other team may be shooting from a hiding spot. Snipers try to surprise other players.

Players have to watch out for snipers.

A tape runner stays by the edge of the playing field.

TAPE RUNNERS AND ROVERS

Players may be tape runners. They move to the edge of the field. Tape runners have to watch for opponents only on one side.

Tape runners are often shot at. They try to find a place to hide and shoot at the other team. They try to keep moving forward along the tape.

Other players are rovers. They go where they are needed. Rovers can help players who are in trouble. They can join a group to capture a flag. Rovers can also help defend their team's flag.

WATCH OUT

Players can try to fool each other. One trick is the dead man's walk. A player may start to walk off the field, looking disappointed. Other players may think this player has been hit. The player then quickly tries to mark other players.

A player also has to watch for friendly fire. Friendly fire is a shot by one's own teammates. Players are out even if they get hit by friendly fire.

EDGE FACT

The time limit for a game depends on the number of players and the size of the field. A game can last 10 minutes, a few hours, or a whole day.

With the dead man's walk, a player pretends to be hit, then opens fire.

CHAPTER 4

PLAYERS AND LEAGUES

Most people play paintball for fun. Some people play pro paintball. Both amateur and pro players can compete in tournaments.

AMATEUR PAINTBALL

College paintball players compete in National Collegiate Paintball Association (NCPA) events. This group sponsors 20 events each season. The University of Illinois won the first four NCPA National Championships.

LEARN ABOUT:

- College paintball
- Tournaments
- NXL

College students compete against each other in NCPA tournaments.

The International Amateur Open is held every summer in Pittsburgh. This tournament is for players who are not pros. At least 1,000 players participate in the five-day event. Teams can win money or prizes.

The Skyball tournament is played in the SkyDome in Toronto. More than 200 teams compete for thousands of dollars in prizes. Skyball is the world's largest five-player team tournament.

PROFESSIONAL PAINTBALL

The National X Ball League (NXL) was formed in 2003. This pro league has eight teams. An NXL game has two 25-minute halves. Each team tries to capture the flag and bring it back to its flag station as many times as possible.

There are two pro paintball circuits. Paintball Sports Promotions (PSP) hosts NXL events. PSP events have games with either five or 10 players. The NXL teams compete at PSP events. The

EDGE FACT

The NXL champions in 2003 were the Philadelphia Americans.

National Professional Paintball League (NPPL) has seven-player events.

Paintball is a new sport, but it's growing fast. It's safer than many people think. Paintball injuries are rare when players wear the proper gear. People enjoy the safe danger of this exciting sport.

NXL games are played all over the United States.

GLOSSARY

amateur (AM-uh-chur)—an athlete who does not earn a living from competing in a sport

ambush (AM-bush)—to hide and then attack someone

camouflage (KAM-uh-flahzh)—coloring or covering that makes animals, people, and objects blend in with their surroundings

carbon dioxide (KAR-buhn dye-OK-side)—a gas found naturally in the air; carbon dioxide has no smell or color; it does not burn.

gelatin (JEL-uh-tuhn)—a clear substance used in making jelly, desserts, and glue

rover (ROH-vuhr)—a player who goes to any position on the field

skirmish (SKUR-mish)—a minor fight in a battle

sniper (SNIPE-uhr)—a player who shoots at other players from a hiding place

squeegee (SKWEE-jee)—a tool used to clean a broken paintball out of a paintgun

READ MORE

Davidson, Steve, et al. *The Complete Guide to Paintball.* Long Island City, N.Y.: Hatherleigh Press, 2002.

Little, John R., and Curtis F. Wong, eds. *Ultimate Guide to Paintball.* Lincolnwood, Ill.: Contemporary Books, 2001.

INTERNET SITES

FactHound offers a safe, fun way to find Internet sites related to this book. All of the sites on FactHound have been researched by our staff.

Here's how:

1. Visit *www.facthound.com*
2. Type in this special code **0736827110** for age-appropriate sites. Or enter a search word related to this book for a more general search.
3. Click on the **Fetch It** button.

FactHound will fetch the best sites for you!

INDEX